D1448053

WHALES
WORK TOGETHER

CLARA COLEMAN

PowerKiDS
press™

New York

Published in 2018 by The Rosen Publishing Group, Inc.
29 East 21st Street, New York, NY 10010

First Edition

Editor: Melissa Raé Shofner
Book Design: Michael J. Flynn

Photo Credits: Cover John Hyde/Perspectives/Getty Images; p. 5 Rodrigo Friscione/Cultura/Getty Images; p. 7 hecke61/Shutterstock.com; p. 8 oksana.perkins/Shutterstock.com; p. 9 Pop Navy/Shutterstock.com; pp. 10–11 Franco Banfi/WaterFrame/Getty Images; p. 12 Dmytro Pylypenko/Shutterstock.com; p. 13 Mark Carwardine/Photolibrary/Getty Images; p. 15 Yann hubert/Shutterstock.com; p. 17 Tomas Kotouc/Shutterstock.com; p. 19 Willyam Bradberry/Shutterstock.com; p. 21 Hiroya Minakuchi/Minden Pictures/Getty Images; p. 22 Billy Blue Photography/Shutterstock.com.

Library of Congress Cataloging-in-Publication Data

Names: Coleman, Clara O., author.
Title: Whales work together / Clara Coleman.
Description: New York : PowerKids Press, [2018] | Series: Animal teamwork |
  Includes index.
Identifiers: LCCN 2017013035| ISBN 9781508155508 (pbk. book) | ISBN
  9781508155324 (6 pack) | ISBN 9781508155447 (library bound book)
Subjects: LCSH: Whales–Behavior–Juvenile literature.
Classification: LCC QL737.C4 C575 2018 | DDC 599.53–dc23
LC record available at https://lccn.loc.gov/2017013035

Manufactured in the United States of America

CPSIA Compliance Information: Batch #BS17PK: For Further Information contact Rosen Publishing, New York, New York at 1-800-237-9932

CONTENTS

WHALES OF THE WORLD

Many kinds and sizes of whales live in the world's oceans. Whales are some of the biggest animals on the planet. Some are longer than a school bus. Imagine seeing a group, or pod, of these **marine** giants!

Whale watchers know how cool it is to spot a pod of whales. These huge animals sometimes jump out of the water and land with a big splash! Whales sometimes use teamwork when hunting and raising their young.

CRITTER COOPERATION

Whales are closely **related** to dolphins and porpoises. Believe it or not, all these marine mammals have a tiny bit of hair on their bodies when they're born.

Whales aren't fish—they're mammals. Mammals are warm-blooded animals with a backbone. Mammals also have hair or fur and give birth to live young that they feed with milk they make in their body.

WHERE THEY LIVE

Whales live in ocean waters around the world. Some species, or kinds, prefer warm waters, but others live comfortably in Earth's coldest waters. Some species live in shallow coastal waters, while others prefer the deep sea.

Many types of whales move around from one area to another to find food or a **mate** and to have babies. This is called migration. Whale migrations can include several pods all working together to get where they need to go. Most pods have 2 to 30 whales, but some have hundreds.

CRITTER COOPERATION

Whales can swim up to 30 miles (48.3 km) per hour. Some species can stay underwater for up to 90 minutes!

Humpback whales have one of the longest migrations of any animal. Some humpbacks migrate more than 10,000 miles (16,093.4 km) round trip!

PARTS OF A WHALE

All whales have flippers and flukes. Flukes, or tail fins, help whales move through the water. Flippers are paddle-like fins on their sides that help whales turn. Whales have lungs. They breathe air through a blowhole on top of their head. This allows them to stay underwater longer.

There are two main groups of whales: baleen and toothed. Baleen whales don't have teeth in their mouth. Instead, they have baleen, which are special plates with **bristles**, sort of like giant toothbrushes.

Toothed whales have one blowhole.
Baleen whales have two.

BALEEN

CRITTER COOPERATION

Whales have a thick layer of fat called blubber under their skin. Blubber helps keep them warm.

HUNTING WITH TEETH

Toothed whales—such as sperm whales and beaked whales—have teeth. They hunt for animals such as squid, skates, sharks, and fish.

Sperm whales may use teamwork while they hunt. They also work together to raise their young.

CRITTER COOPERATION

Sperm whales are the largest toothed animals on Earth. Male sperm whales can grow up to about 59 feet (18 m) long and weigh 45 tons (40.8 mt). Females are usually much smaller.

Sperm whales live and hunt in the deep sea. Scientists think they may work together to catch **prey**. In a recent study, they noticed some sperm whales would herd schools of squid into groups while others dove in for a meal. This is sometimes called carousel feeding. Killer whales, which are actually dolphins, are also known to work together this way.

FILTERING FOOD

Baleen whales, such as blue whales and humpback whales, use baleen to **filter** very small creatures from seawater. They mostly eat krill but may also eat **plankton** and small fish.

Humpback whales sometimes surround schools of small fish and blow bubbles from their blowholes. This "bubble net" causes the fish to group together and rise toward the surface. The humpbacks swim to the surface for a quick, large meal. They can eat up to 3,000 pounds (1,360.8 kg) of food every day!

Krill are tiny crustaceans found in all of Earth's oceans. Crustaceans are animals with a hard shell, two pairs of feelers, and three body segments, or parts. Lobsters, crabs, and shrimp are also crustaceans.

KRILL

CRITTER COOPERATION

Blue whales are the largest animals ever to live on Earth. They can grow to 105 feet (32 m) long and weigh more than 200 tons (181.4 mt). You might be surprised to hear that this giant animal eats some of the smallest creatures on the planet—krill.

IT'S A WHALE'S LIFE

Whale life cycles are similar to human life cycles. Baby whales, called calves, look just like adults, but they're smaller. Depending on the species, it can take a whale between 6 and 15 years to reach adulthood.

Whale mothers take good care of calves. Whale sisters, aunts, and grandmothers also care for the young, as do other female members of the pod. These whales often form lifelong relationships. Some whales get along better than others.

CRITTER COOPERATION

Depending on the species, whales can live for 30 to 100 years or more. Bowhead whales can live to be 200 years old! That makes them the longest-living mammals on Earth.

Many whale species, such as these humpback whales, form close-knit families with lifelong relationships. However, males usually leave the pod when they're young and may never see their original family again.

LEARNING FROM EACH OTHER

Many whales migrate between where they like to eat and where they have their babies. Some species, such as humpbacks, return to the same place each year to feed. Scientists think humpbacks teach their calves where the best feeding grounds are.

When a whale is born, it needs to learn to swim right away. It also needs air to breathe. A calf's mother will help it find the surface by gently pushing it upward. Sometimes aunts or other whales in the pod will help.

CRITTER COOPERATION

While the relationship between a mother and her calf is strong, humpback whales don't usually form long-lasting relationships. Most only know each other for a few days.

Some whales, such as humpbacks, are known to jump from the water and land, often on their back. This is called breaching. Scientists aren't sure why whales breach, but they believe young whales learn to do it by copying older whales.

17

TALKING UNDERWATER

Many whale species form pods that stay together for a long time. Even if a whale leaves a pod, the members may still recognize that whale many years later. Scientists think the sounds whales make help them remember each other.

Whales **communicate** with each other in several ways. They will often use clicks to find food. Whales may whistle to their friends. They also groan, sigh, and squeak. Some whale noises sound like songs. Males use low songs to find mates.

CRITTER COOPERATION

Scientists think pods of whales might have different **dialects**, even when the whales are of the same species. This may help whales figure out which whales they know and which are strangers.

Whales sometimes slap their tail or flippers on the surface of the water. Sometimes they do this to scare fish into a group. Sometimes it's a sign of **aggression**.

19

BELUGAS AND ECHOLOCATION

Beluga whales make a lot of noise. They use many different sounds to talk to each other. Young belugas learn how to communicate from their mothers, aunts, and sisters. Scientists think they learn much like human babies do, using simple noises that become more **complex** over time.

Like other toothed whales, belugas use **echolocation** to help them move around their watery world. Echolocation helps toothed whales find prey and avoid objects underwater. Using echolocation, whales can "see" things several miles away.

CRITTER COOPERATION

Unlike most other types of whales, belugas are able to move their neck quite well and can turn their head in all directions.

Recent studies suggest belugas may also communicate by blowing different types of bubbles to show how they feel. They'll blow bubble rings for fun and to socialize. Sometimes belugas will blow matching rings or try to pop each other's bubbles.

HUMAN INTERFERENCE

Sound travels through water very well. This is why whales can hear each other and "see" objects using echolocation from far away. Unfortunately, humans make a lot of noise, too.

Sonar is a big problem for whales. It interferes, or gets in the way, of the normal sounds they make to communicate. This makes it hard for whales to find mates, and they may get lost while migrating. To help whales, there are laws to limit the use of sonar in certain areas.

GLOSSARY

aggression: Forceful or angry actions.

bristles: Short, stiff hair or fibers.

communicate: To share ideas and feelings through sounds and motions.

complex: Having many parts.

dialect: Different ways that a language is spoken in different areas.

echolocation: A method of locating objects by producing a sound and judging the distance and location by the time it takes the echo to return.

filter: To remove items from a liquid or gas by passing that liquid or gas through something with tiny openings.

marine: Having to do with the sea.

mate: One of two animals that come together to make babies.

plankton: Tiny plants and animals that float freely in water.

prey: An animal hunted by other animals for food.

related: Belonging to the same group or family because of shared qualities.

sonar: A machine or method that uses sound waves to find things in a body of water.

INDEX

WEBSITES

Due to the changing nature of Internet links, PowerKids Press has developed an online list of websites related to the subject of this book. This site is updated regularly. Please use this link to access the list: www.powerkidslinks.com/atw/whal